just us guys

just us guys

A Journal for Dads and Sons

R

ROCKRIDGE
PRESS

For general information on our other products and services or to obtain technical support, please contact our Customer Care Department within the United States at (866) 744-2665, or outside the United States at (510) 253-0500.

Rockridge Press publishes its books in a variety of electronic and print formats. Some content that appears in print may not be available in electronic books, and vice versa.

TRADEMARKS: Rockridge Press and the Rockridge Press logo are trademarks or registered trademarks of Callisto Media Inc. and/or its affiliates, in the United States and other countries, and may not be used without written permission. All other trade-marks are the property of their respective owners. Rockridge Press is not associated with any product or vendor mentioned in this book.

Series Designer: Erin Yeung
Interior and Cover Designer: Karmen Lizzul
Art Producer: Tom Hood
Editor: John Makowski
Production Editor: Dylan Julian
Production Manager: Riley Hoffman

All illustrations used under license from istock.com

Paperback ISBN: 978-1-63878-101-1
R0

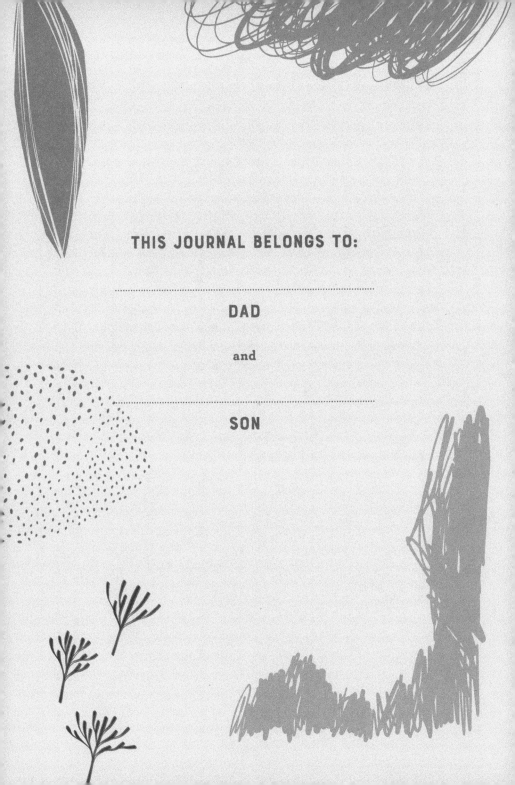

THIS JOURNAL BELONGS TO:

....

DAD

and

....

SON

GETTING STARTED

Welcome to *Just Us Guys: A Journal for Dads and Sons*! Journaling together will allow you to learn new things about each other by inspiring you to ask questions you might not have asked otherwise. This experience will bring you closer together.

This journal is a truly interactive way to capture your father-son relationship. There's plenty of space for you to jot down your reflections every day. Short-answer prompts open a window onto how each of you thinks, while long-form questions offer opportunities for deeper conversation about topics relevant to both of you. And plenty of free-writing pages allow you to expand on your answers or talk about other issues that are important to you.

These prompts—some light and fun, some deep and thought-provoking—will help you learn each other's hopes and dreams, share thoughts about the family and making friends, and discover some special skills and talents you both possess. Get started on your year of journaling together by setting some expectations in the "Beginning of the Year" section. And, at the end, the "Reflecting on the Year" section will allow you to reflect on all that you've learned about each other.

To get the most out of this journal:

Take your time. Don't feel you have to rush through a month's prompts all during the first week. If you need more time during any section of the journal, just make sure your writing partner knows.

Listen without judging. You will be learning things about each other that you didn't know before, and you might have a difference of opinion. That's the beauty of journaling together. Keep an open mind and respect each other's differences.

Be honest. Don't feel like you have to hide anything or hold back. Journaling together is an opportunity for you to say everything you've ever wanted to say to each other. Let it all out.

Use kind words. You can be honest and still be respectful. Have you ever heard the saying "You can get more flies with honey than vinegar"? Using kind words when you're writing about difficult subjects makes the message or question a lot easier to receive.

Create a long-distance plan. If one of you is traveling or you don't live together, you can pick the prompts you'll write about ahead of time and send them to each other in a letter or via email. You can even text your answers. It would be fun to use these prompts as inspiration for conversation during telephone calls or video chats.

Make this journal your own. If the tips for using this journal don't work for you, do whatever will make the experience more meaningful to you. This is your journal and your experience. Have a good time on this journey!

BEGINNING OF THE YEAR

Before you start, set aside some time to sit down together and lay out your expectations for how you'll use this journal. You'll both be happy to know where your journaling fits in. Answer these questions honestly. Consider all your obligations so you'll have realistic expectations for each other. Once you answer these questions, you'll be all set to jump in and get started!

WE STARTED THIS JOURNAL TOGETHER ON

....

A PICTURE OF US AT THE BEGINNING OF THE YEAR

1. Why are we writing in this journal together?

....

....

....

2. When will we write in this journal? Will we do it every day? Once a week?

....

....

....

3. How much time do we need for each entry?

....

....

....

4. Should we plan time to talk afterward?

....

....

....

....

5. Will we go through the journal in order or skip around?

....

....

....

6. How will we decide which entries to complete and when?

....

....

....

7. What could we do if we need more space to write?

....

....

....

8. What do we want to learn about each other by doing this journal?

....

....

....

....

MONTH ONE

· ·

The thing I love most about myself is:

....

....

You can tell when I'm in a silly mood because I:

....

....

If you want me to laugh like crazy, do this:

....

....

When I'm sad, I:

....

....

This week, I worried about:

....

....

....

DAD

The thing I love most about myself is:

....

....

You can tell when I'm in a silly mood because I:

....

....

If you want me to laugh like crazy, do this:

....

....

When I'm sad, I:

....

....

This week, I worried about:

....

....

....

....

SON

What's something about you that you think I don't know?

DAD

What's something about you that you think I don't know?

SON

Three things I want to know about you:

1. ....
2. ....
3. ....

My answers to the things you want to know about me:

....
....
....
....
....
....
....
....
....
....
....
....
....

DAD

Three things I want to know about you:

1. ....

2. ....

3. ....

My answers to the things you want to know about me:

....

....

....

....

....

....

....

....

....

....

....

....

....

....

....

....

SON

This is something I'm really good at:

....

....

This is something I do well, but I don't like to do:

....

....

This is something I wish I had more time to do:

....

....

Two goals I have for the year ahead are:

....

....

This is how I plan to achieve those goals:

....

....

....

DAD

This is something I'm really good at:

....

....

This is something I do well, but I don't like to do:

....

....

This is something I wish I had more time to do:

....

....

Two goals I have for the year ahead are:

....

....

This is how I plan to achieve those goals:

....

....

....

SON

Share a secret talent that you have.

What's your favorite way to be creative?

DAD

Share a secret talent that you have.

What's your favorite way to be creative?

SON

How did you feel when you learned you were going to be the dad of a son?

....

....

....

....

....

....

....

....

....

....

....

....

....

....

....

DAD

What was a decision I made as a dad that you didn't agree with? What would you have done instead?

....

....

....

....

....

....

....

....

....

....

....

....

....

....

....

....

....

SON

FREE-WRITING SPACE

DAD

FREE-WRITING SPACE

SON

MONTH TWO

What's it really like to be an adult? What do you like, and what don't you like?

....

....

....

....

....

....

....

My thoughts on what you wrote about being a teenager:

....

....

....

....

....

....

....

....

DAD

What's it like being a teenager today? What do you like, and
what don't you like?

....

....

....

....

....

....

....

My thoughts on what you wrote about being an adult:

....

....

....

....

....

....

....

....

SON

If I could add one quality to our relationship, it would be

.... because:

....

....

....

If you could plan the perfect day for us, what would it look like?

....

....

....

The best thing that happened to me this week was:

....

....

My favorite dad-and-son pair in pop culture is ....

.... because:

....

....

....

DAD

If I could add one quality to our relationship, it would be

.... because:

....

....

....

If you could plan the perfect day for us, what would it look like?

....

....

....

The best thing that happened to me this week was:

....

....

My favorite dad-and-son pair in pop culture is ....

.... because:

....

....

....

SON

More money or more friends. Which would you choose? Why?

....

....

....

....

....

....

....

....

When I think about the future, I feel ....

.... because:

....

....

....

....

....

....

DAD

More money or more friends. Which would you choose? Why?

....
....
....
....
....
....
....
....

When I think about the future, I feel ....
.... because:

....
....
....
....
....
....

SON

Share what a day in your life is like.

What's your favorite way to spend downtime?

DAD

Share what a day in your life is like.

What's your favorite way to spend downtime?

SON

One person in our family I wish I were closer to is ....
.... because:

_____

_____

_____

_____

_____

_____

_____

_____

_____

_____

_____

_____

_____

_____

DAD

One person in our family I wish I were closer to is ....because:

....

....

....

....

....

....

....

....

....

....

....

....

....

....

....

SON

FREE-WRITING SPACE

DAD

FREE-WRITING SPACE

SON

MONTH THREE

· ·

Right now, this is the thing I'm most intensely focused on:

....

....

This is something that recently stressed me out:

....

....

Tell me about a good book you read or movie you saw
recently.

....

....

....

....

Tell me about something weird or interesting that you
recently learned all about.

....

....

....

....

....

DAD

Right now, this is the thing I'm most intensely focused on:

....

....

This is something that recently stressed me out:

....

....

Tell me about a good book you read or movie you saw recently.

....

....

....

....

Tell me about something weird or interesting that you recently learned all about.

....

....

....

....

....

SON

What's something important to you that you want
me to care about, too, and how can I be involved?

....

....

....

....

....

....

....

....

My thoughts on your response:

....

....

....

....

....

....

....

....

DAD

What's something important to you that you want
me to care about, too, and how can I be involved?

....

....

....

....

....

....

....

My thoughts on your response:

....

....

....

....

....

....

....

....

SON

Six things I tried and didn't like:

1. ....

2. ....

3. ....

4. ....

5. ....

6. ....

Six things I tried and liked:

1. ....

2. ....

3. ....

4. ....

5. ....

6. ....

DAD

Six things I tried and didn't like:

1. ....
2. ....
3. ....
4. ....
5. ....
6. ....

Six things I tried and liked:

1. ....
2. ....
3. ....
4. ....
5. ....
6. ....

SON

If I didn't have work and other responsibilities, this is what I would do all day:

....

....

....

....

....

At your age, I thought adulthood would be:

....

....

....

....

These are the most surprising things about being an adult:

....

....

....

....

....

DAD

If I didn't have school and other responsibilities, this is what I would do all day:

....

....

....

....

....

This is what I like most about growing up:

....

....

....

....

These are the ways it's different from how I thought it would be:

....

....

....

....

....

SON

Do you think of yourself as a dreamer? Why or why not?

DAD

Do you think of yourself as a dreamer? Why or why not?

SON

FREE-WRITING SPACE

DAD

FREE-WRITING SPACE

SON

MONTH FOUR

Tell me about a time when you put in extra effort and your hard work paid off. How did you feel?

....

....

....

....

....

....

When you were little, what kind of work did you want to do? How is your work now different from or similar to what you imagined you would be doing when you were a child?

....

....

....

....

....

....

....

....

....

DAD

Tell me about a time when you put in extra effort and your hard work paid off. How did you feel?

....

....

....

....

....

....

When you grow up, what kind of work do you want to do? What kind of feeling do you want to get from your work?

....

....

....

....

....

....

....

....

....

SON

If you could be a kid forever or an adult forever, which would you choose and why?

DAD

If you could be a kid forever or an adult forever, which would you choose and why?

SON

Six things that make me special:

1. ....
2. ....
3. ....
4. ....
5. ....
6. ....

Six things that make you special:

1. ....
2. ....
3. ....
4. ....
5. ....
6. ....

DAD

Six things that make me special:

1. ....

2. ....

3. ....

4. ....

5. ....

6. ....

Six things that make you special:

1. ....

2. ....

3. ....

4. ....

5. ....

6. ....

SON

This is the actor who would play me in a movie of our lives:

....

This is the actor who would play you in a movie of our lives:

....

I love when you and I...

together, because:...

....

....

The most fun we had together recently was when we:

....

....

Besides spending time with you, I really enjoy spending

time with ....because:

....

....

....

....

DAD

This is the actor who would play me in a movie of our lives:

....

This is the actor who would play you in a movie of our lives:

....

I love when you and I ....

together, because: ....

....

....

The most fun we had together recently was when we:

....

....

Besides spending time with you, I really enjoy spending

time with .... because:

....

....

....

....

SON

Who's inspired you lately to be more kind?

....

What did they do or say that motivated you?

....

....

....

....

....

....

Tell me about the nicest thing you've ever done for
someone else.

....

....

....

....

....

....

....

DAD

Who's inspired you lately to be more kind?

....

What did they do or say that motivated you?

....

....

....

....

....

....

Tell me about the nicest thing you've ever done for someone else.

....

....

....

....

....

....

....

SON

FREE-WRITING SPACE

DAD

FREE-WRITING SPACE

SON

MONTH FIVE

If I were a superhero, my name would be:

....

My superpower would be:

....

The last time I tried something new, I:

....

....

I am proud of myself for:

....

....

....

This is something I wish I had done differently:

....

....

....

....

DAD

If I were a superhero, my name would be:

....

My superpower would be:

....

The last time I tried something new, I:

....

....

I am proud of myself for:

....

....

....

This is something I wish I had done differently:

....

....

....

....

SON

Make an anagram of your name.

....

Do you like your name? Why or why not? If not, what would you want it to be?

....

....

....

....

....

....

Tell me the story of how you chose my name, and why.

....

....

....

....

....

....

DAD

Make an anagram of your name.

....

Do you like your name? Why or why not?

....

....

....

....

....

....

....

If you got to choose your own name, what would it be
and why?

....

....

....

....

....

....

....

SON

When you do this, it reminds me of myself, because:

....

....

....

....

....

....

....

I wish I had been like you in this way when I was younger, because:

....

....

....

....

....

....

....

....

DAD

When you do this, it reminds me of myself, because:

....

....

....

....

....

....

....

I hope I am like you in this way when I am older,
because:

....

....

....

....

....

....

....

....

SON

You're a wonderful son because:

....

....

....

....

....

....

....

....

....

....

....

....

....

....

....

....

DAD

I like having you as my dad because:

....

....

....

....

....

....

....

....

....

....

....

....

....

....

....

....

....

SON

What's something you've done as a dad that you thought you'd never do?

....

....

....

....

What made you change your mind?

....

....

....

How do you feel about the change?

....

....

....

....

....

....

....

DAD

What's something that you changed your mind about recently?

....
....
....
....

What made you change your mind?

....
....
....

How do you feel about the change?

....
....
....
....
....
....
....
....

SON

FREE-WRITING SPACE

DAD

FREE-WRITING SPACE

SON

MONTH SIX

What's something that put you in a good mood this week?

....

....

....

What's something you're looking forward to?

....

....

....

....

For my next birthday, I want to celebrate by:

....

....

....

....

....

....

....

....

DAD

What's something that put you in a good mood this week?

....

....

....

What's something you're looking forward to?

....

....

....

....

For my next birthday, I want to celebrate by:

....

....

....

....

....

....

....

....

SON

What would your friends say if they were describing you to someone who didn't know you?

....

....

....

....

....

....

....

Share the most embarrassing thing that happened to you when you were a kid.

....

....

....

....

....

....

....

....

DAD

What would your friends say if they were describing you to someone who didn't know you?

....
....
....
....
....
....
....

Tell me about a time when you were embarrassed in front of your friends.

....
....
....
....
....
....
....
....

SON

My favorite sight is..because:

....

....

My favorite sound is..because:

....

....

My favorite smell is..because:

....

....

My favorite taste is..because:

....

....

The one sentimental possession I could never get rid of is

....because:

....

....

....

DAD

My favorite sight is.. because:

....

....

My favorite sound is.. because:

....

....

My favorite smell is.. because:

....

....

My favorite taste is.. because:

....

....

The one sentimental possession I could never get rid of is

.... because:

....

....

....

SON

Do you prefer being around lots of people or having alone time? Why?

....

....

....

....

....

....

....

Do you find it easy or hard to make friends? Why?

....

....

....

....

....

....

....

....

DAD

Do you prefer being around lots of people or having alone time? Why?

....
....
....
....
....
....
....

Do you find it easy or hard to make friends? Why?

....
....
....
....
....
....
....
....

SON

FREE-WRITING SPACE

DAD

FREE-WRITING SPACE

SON

MONTH SEVEN

· ·

My best friends are .... because:

....
....
....

These are the qualities I value in a friend:

....
....
....
....
....
....

These are the ways I want to be a better friend:

....
....
....
....
....
....
....

DAD

My best friends are ....because:

....

....

....

These are the qualities I value in a friend:

....

....

....

....

....

....

These are the ways I want to be a better friend:

....

....

....

....

....

....

....

SON

When you were my age, who was your best friend?

....

....

....

....

....

....

....

My longest friendship is with ...., and

the reasons we've been able to stay friends for so long are:

....

....

....

....

....

....

....

DAD

How would you describe me to your friends?

....

....

....

....

....

....

....

....

My longest friendship is with ...., and
the reasons we've been able to stay friends for so long are:

....

....

....

....

....

....

....

....

....

SON

These are some assumptions people have about me:

....
....
....
....
....

They make me feel:

....
....
....
....
....

I wish more people knew this fact about me:

....
....
....
....
....

DAD

These are some assumptions people have about me:

....

....

....

....

....

They make me feel:

....

....

....

....

....

I wish more people knew this fact about me:

....

....

....

....

....

....

SON

The naughtiest thing I ever did was:

....

....

....

Why did you do it, and did you suffer any consequences?
If so, what?

....

....

....

....

....

....

....

....

....

....

....

DAD

The naughtiest thing I ever did was:

....

....

....

Why did you do it, and did you suffer any consequences?
If so, what?

....

....

....

....

....

....

....

....

....

....

....

....

SON

What's something you wish you could get a second chance at, and why?

What would you do differently?

DAD

What's something you wish you could get a second chance at, and why?

....
....
....
....
....
....
....

What would you do differently?

....
....
....
....
....
....
....
....

SON

FREE-WRITING SPACE

DAD

FREE-WRITING SPACE

SON

MONTH EIGHT

My favorite tradition of ours is ....

because: ....

....

....

....

Do you think work and school get in the way of "us time"?
Why or why not?

....

....

....

Some suggestions I have for making more time for us are:

....

....

....

....

....

....

....

....

DAD

My favorite tradition of ours is..

because:..

....

....

....

Do you think work and school get in the way of "us time"?
Why or why not?

....

....

....

Some suggestions I have for making more time for us are:

....

....

....

....

....

....

....

....

SON

Sometimes you hurt my feelings when you do this:

....
....
....
....
....

Whenever we have a disagreement, I feel:

....
....
....
....

When we have an argument, this is my favorite way to make up:

....
....
....
....
....

DAD

Sometimes you hurt my feelings when you do this:

....

....

....

....

....

Whenever we have a disagreement, I feel:

....

....

....

....

When we have an argument, this is my favorite way to make up:

....

....

....

....

....

....

SON

Tell me about a time you argued with someone close to you. What caused the disagreement and how did you resolve it?

DAD

Tell me about a time you argued with someone close to you.
What caused the disagreement and how did you resolve it?

SON

If I were in charge of everybody, I would make these laws:

....

....

....

....

....

....

If you had a million dollars and had to spend it all in one
day, what would you do?

....

....

....

....

....

....

....

....

....

....

....

DAD

If I were in charge of everybody, I would make these laws:

....

....

....

....

....

....

If you had a million dollars and had to spend it all in one day, what would you do?

....

....

....

....

....

....

....

....

....

....

....

SON

Tell me about someone in our family I don't know or don't know well.

DAD

Tell me about a friend or teacher I don't know or don't know well.

SON

FREE-WRITING SPACE

DAD

FREE-WRITING SPACE

SON

MONTH NINE

These are the books, TV shows, movies, and activities
I want to complete:

....

....

....

....

....

....

....

....

....

....

....

....

....

....

....

....

DAD

These are the books, TV shows, movies, and activities
I want to complete:

....

....

....

....

....

....

....

....

....

....

....

....

....

....

....

....

....

....

....

SON

Can dads and sons be friends? Why or why not?

....

....

....

....

....

....

This is my response to what you wrote about dads and sons being friends:

....

....

....

....

....

....

....

DAD

Can dads and sons be friends? Why or why not?

....

....

....

....

....

....

....

This is my response to what you wrote about dads and sons being friends:

....

....

....

....

....

....

....

....

SON

If I could be something other than human, I'd be ....

.... because:

....

....

....

Do you ever wish you could switch places with me? Why or why not?

....

....

....

....

....

If we did switch places, I'd do these things:

....

....

....

....

....

....

DAD

If I could be something other than human, I'd be ....

.... because:

....

....

....

Do you ever wish you could switch places with me? Why or why not?

....

....

....

....

....

If we did switch places, I'd do these things:

....

....

....

....

....

....

SON

Ten things I'm grateful for right now:

1. ....

....

2. ....

....

3. ....

....

4. ....

....

5. ....

....

6. ....

....

7. ....

....

8. ....

....

9. ....

....

10. ....

....

DAD

Ten things I'm grateful for right now:

1. ....
   ....

2. ....
   ....

3. ....
   ....

4. ....
   ....

5. ....
   ....

6. ....
   ....

7. ....
   ....

8. ....
   ....

9. ....
   ....

10. ....
    ....

SON

Tell me a story about your first romantic relationship.

....
....
....
....
....
....
....
....

What are some things you want me to know about dating and falling in love?

....
....
....
....
....
....
....
....

DAD

Do you and your friends talk about dating? What do you talk about? What do you want to know about dating and falling in love?

SON

FREE-WRITING SPACE

DAD

FREE-WRITING SPACE

SON

MONTH TEN

If we were to host a talk show together, it would be called
...., and our
theme song would sound like this:

....

....

Do you think I appreciate you? Why or why not?

....

....

What's something I could do to show my appreciation for
you more often?

....

....

....

The next time we have a day together, let's:

....

....

....

DAD

If we were to host a talk show together, it would be called

...., and our

theme song would sound like this:

....

....

Do you think I appreciate you? Why or why not?

....

....

What's something I could do to show my appreciation for you more often?

....

....

....

The next time we have a day together, let's:

....

....

....

SON

If you were going to run for president, what would your platform be?

....

....

....

....

....

What's one social issue that's really important to you? Why do you care about it so much?

....

....

....

....

If there was one thing I could change right now about the world we live in, it would be:

....

....

....

....

DAD

If you were going to run for president, what would your platform be?

....

....

....

....

....

What's one social issue that's really important to you? Why do you care about it so much?

....

....

....

....

If there was one thing I could change right now about the world we live in, it would be:

....

....

....

....

SON

What's the best advice you ever received, and who shared it with you?

....

....

....

....

....

....

....

How have you put that advice into practice?

....

....

....

....

....

....

....

....

DAD

What's the best advice you ever received, and who shared it with you?

....
....
....
....
....
....
....
....

How have you put that advice into practice?

....
....
....
....
....
....
....
....

SON

What's one dream goal you want to accomplish?

....

....

....

....

....

....

....

How would you accomplish this goal?

....

....

....

....

....

....

....

....

....

DAD

What's one dream goal you want to accomplish?

....

....

....

....

....

....

....

How would you accomplish this goal?

....

....

....

....

....

....

....

....

....

SON

If you could go back in time and tell your past self anything,
what would it be and why?

....

....

....

....

....

....

....

....

....

....

....

....

....

....

....

....

DAD

What lesson have you learned recently that you think will really help you in the future as an adult, and why?

....

....

....

....

....

....

....

....

....

....

....

....

....

....

....

....

....

SON

FREE-WRITING SPACE

DAD

FREE-WRITING SPACE

SON

MONTH ELEVEN

If I had to live on a desert island, these are four things
I'd bring:

1. ....

2. ....

3. ....

4. ....

If I could eat only three foods for the rest of my life, they
would be:

1. ....

2. ....

3. ....

If I could try four careers without having to commit, they
would be:

1. ....

2. ....

3. ....

4. ....

DAD

If I had to live on a desert island, these are four things I'd bring:

1. ....

2. ....

3. ....

4. ....

If I could eat only three foods for the rest of my life, they would be:

1. ....

2. ....

3. ....

If I could try four careers without having to commit, they would be:

1. ....

2. ....

3. ....

4. ....

SON

Tell me about a time when you were wrong about something. What was the situation? How did you handle it? What did you do when you realized you were wrong?

DAD

Tell me about a time when you didn't handle a problem appropriately. What happened? What would you do differently?

....

....

....

....

....

....

....

....

....

....

....

....

....

....

....

....

....

....

SON

The title of my autobiography would be:

....

The celebrity I would change places with is:

....

My favorite age so far is .... because:

....

....

....

The best gift I ever received was ....

because: ....

....

....

....

....

....

....

....

DAD

The title of my autobiography would be:

....

The celebrity I would change places with is:

....

My favorite age so far is .... because:

....

....

....

The best gift I ever received was ....

because: ....

....

....

....

....

....

....

....

SON

What's something you've learned from me but have never told me?

....

....

....

....

....

....

....

This is what I've learned from you:

....

....

....

....

....

....

....

....

DAD

What's something you've learned from me but have never told me?

....

....

....

....

....

....

....

....

This is what I've learned from you:

....

....

....

....

....

....

....

....

SON

Tell me about the most magical or unexpected experience you've ever had.

DAD

Tell me about the most magical or unexpected experience you've ever had.

SON

FREE-WRITING SPACE

DAD

FREE-WRITING SPACE

SON

MONTH TWELVE

If you could see into your future, would you want to? Why or why not?

....

....

....

....

If a genie appeared and granted you three wishes, what would they be?

....

....

....

....

If you could speak to someone who has died, who would it be, and what would you want to talk to them about?

....

....

....

....

DAD

If you could see into your future, would you want to? Why or why not?

....
....
....
....
....

If a genie appeared and granted you three wishes, what would they be?

....
....
....
....

If you could speak to someone who has died, who would it be, and what would you want to talk to them about?

....
....
....
....
....

SON

If you could choose to be super smart or super popular, which would you choose, and why?

DAD

If you could choose to be super smart or super popular, which would you choose, and why?

....

....

....

....

....

....

....

....

....

....

....

....

....

....

....

....

SON

Tell me about a time when you had to be a leader. What was the situation? Who did you have to lead? Did people listen to you? What did you learn about leadership?

DAD

Tell me about a time when you had to be in charge. Did you like being in that role? Did people accept you as a leader? What did you learn about being in charge of people from that experience?

....

....

....

....

....

....

....

....

....

....

....

....

....

....

....

SON

I feel insecure about..because:

....

....

....

....

The last time I cried was..because:

....

....

....

....

The last time I was angry was..because:

....

....

....

....

DAD

I feel insecure about .... because:

....

....

....

....

....

The last time I cried was .... because:

....

....

....

....

....

The last time I was angry was .... because:

....

....

....

....

....

....

SON

What I love most about where I grew up is:

....

....

....

....

....

....

....

....

If I could go anywhere in the world, it would be:

....

....

....

....

....

....

....

....

DAD

What I love most about where I grew up is:

....
....
....
....
....
....
....
....

If I could go anywhere in the world, it would be:

....
....
....
....
....
....
....
....

SON

FREE-WRITING SPACE

DAD

FREE-WRITING SPACE

SON

REFLECTING ON THE YEAR

You did it! It's the end of your year of journaling together. The two of you have spent 12 months getting to know each other better. Even though you may have had tough conversations, you've also shared laughs and learned so much more about each other than you knew before.

What do you do now that your journal is complete? Keep asking questions. Continue to be curious about each other. Talk. Listen.

It's awesome to have a special person in your life who cares enough about you to want to know all your likes, dislikes, dreams, and hopes, and to share their own. Never forget what a gift that is.

WE FINISHED THIS JOURNAL TOGETHER ON

....

A PICTURE OF US AT THE END OF THE YEAR

1. Before we started, how did we feel about doing this journal together?

....
....
....
....
....

2. What is our favorite part about having completed this journal together?

....
....
....
....
....

3. What's the most surprising thing we've learned about each other?

....
....
....
....
....

4. How have we changed through journaling together?

....

....

....

....

....

5. How is our relationship different now?

....

....

....

....

....

6. What project would we like to do together next, and when should we begin?

....

....

....

....

....

CPSIA information can be obtained
at www.ICGtesting.com
Printed in the USA
JSHW050427190322
23988JS00001B/1